The Great D

THE FUTURE
OF ENERGY

by Melanie Waldron

raintree

a Capstone company — publishers for children

Engage Literacy is published in the UK by Raintree.
Raintree is an imprint of Capstone Global Library Limited, a company incorporated in England and Wales having its registered office at 264 Banbury Road, Oxford, OX2 7DY – Registered company number: 6695582

www.raintree.co.uk

Editorial credits
Gina Kammer, editor; Rich Parker, designer; Wanda Winch, media researcher,
Steve Walker, production specialist

Image credits
Alamy Stock Photo: PA Images, 30, PNWL, 51; Getty Images Inc: UIG/Auscape, 39; GRID-Arendal: UNEP/Hugo Ahlenius, 19; iStockphoto: dan_prat, 10, MichaelKnudsen, 25, sjo, 57, Newscom: AFLO/TEPCO, 37 (top), imageBROKER/Jim West, 16, Zuma Press/Caters News/Andre Estima, 33; Shutterstock: A. Aleksandravicius, 54–55, Alejo Miranda, 17 (bottom), Alex Mit, cover (middle right), 31, andrey_l, 61, Artwork studio BKK, 34, 41, Ase, electric background design, BigKnell, 20, Choksawatdikorn, 27, Christos Georghiou, 52, denisgo, 53, Drop of Light, 5, Gary Whitton, 6, hfzimages, 60, jhochen, 47, IndustryAndTravel, 14, John T Takai, 17 (top), Kanok Sulaiman, 9, Lena Wurm, 48–49, Lukas Hejtman, 42–43, Mykola Gomeniuk, back cover, 28, pavalena, 21, Peshkova, 62, Radovan1, 18, Ralf Gosch, 23, Ritesh Chaudhary, 58–59, Rudmer Zwerver, cover (middle left), snapgalleria, 29, Soonthorn Wongsaita, cover (top), tele52, 24, Trueffelpix, 11, Ugis Riba, cover (bottom), Ungnoi Lookjeab, 13; Thinkstock: iStockphoto/Gerardo_Borbolla, 44, Stockbyte/Tom Brakefield, 35

21 20
10 9 8 7 6 5 4 3 2 1

The Great Debate: The Future of Energy

ISBN: 978 1 4747 4634 2

Printed and bound in India.

Contents

What is energy?

Energy is everywhere. It makes things move, it provides light and heat and it creates sounds. It keeps us alive, and it allows plants and animals to grow and survive.

We need energy every day. We use it to light and heat our houses, schools and offices. It powers our televisions, cars and computers. When you run around, think, breathe and even when you sleep, your body is using energy.

There are many types of energy. The food we eat every day contains chemical energy, such as sugars. Our bodies change this to other types of energy, such as heat and movement, so we can stay alive and do what we need to do.

Electricity is a type of energy. We use it in our modern world every day, often without thinking about it. It provides the power to make things work.

Although we can't see energy, it is all around us. Think of all the things happening in this picture that use energy.

Humans have been making use of different energy sources for thousands of years. We have made heat and light by burning fuel, such as wood, to make fires. We have used wind to sail boats, and we have used flowing water to grind grain.

For hundreds of years farmers used oxen and horses to do heavy farm work such as pulling ploughs and carts. The animals got their energy from the food the farmers fed them. In many parts of the world today, people still use animals to provide power.

In the 1700s people discovered how to use energy to power machines. They burned coal to boil water and make steam. The steam was piped into machines to make their working parts move. Today, many large *power stations* use steam to create electricity.

In this coal-fired power station, the steam turns machines called *turbines* to create electricity.

What is the debate about energy?

Energy has been in the news a lot over the last few years. We use so much electricity and fuel in our buildings and vehicles that many people worry about the future. This is because we get most of our energy from *fossil fuel*.

Coal, oil and natural gas are fossil fuels. They were formed millions of years ago out of layers of dead plants and animals. These layers were covered, squashed and heated by layers of rock as Earth's surface moved. Over time, they turned into fossil fuels.

POWER FACT

More than 80 per cent of the energy used around the world comes from burning fossil fuels.

Ever since humans found fossil fuel, we have been using it to provide most of our energy. It burns well and makes a lot of heat. We use it in power stations to make electricity. We also use it in vehicles to fuel the engines, and in homes for cooking and heating.

But the discussion on both sides of the issue, or the debate, about energy starts with fossil fuel.

Some oil and gas fields lie in layers of rock under the ocean floor.

The problem with using fossil fuel for most of our energy is that we may run out of it one day. It is known as *non-renewable* fuel. This means that Earth can't make more of it for thousands or even millions of years. If we use it up, there will be none left to provide us with energy.

Tar sand is a sticky mix of thick oil, sand, clay and water. Some oil companies are now opening large tar sand mines to take out the oil.

It is hard to tell how much fossil fuel is left on Earth. This is because much of it lies deep underground, often in far away and remote places. Some scientists think that we may run out of coal in 250 years, gas in 70 years and oil in 50 years. But others disagree with these figures.

As old coal, oil and gas fields are used up, fuel companies look for new ones. They also look for new ways of getting fossil fuel from Earth. By finding new methods, it may be that there are many more years of fossil fuel left than scientists predict.

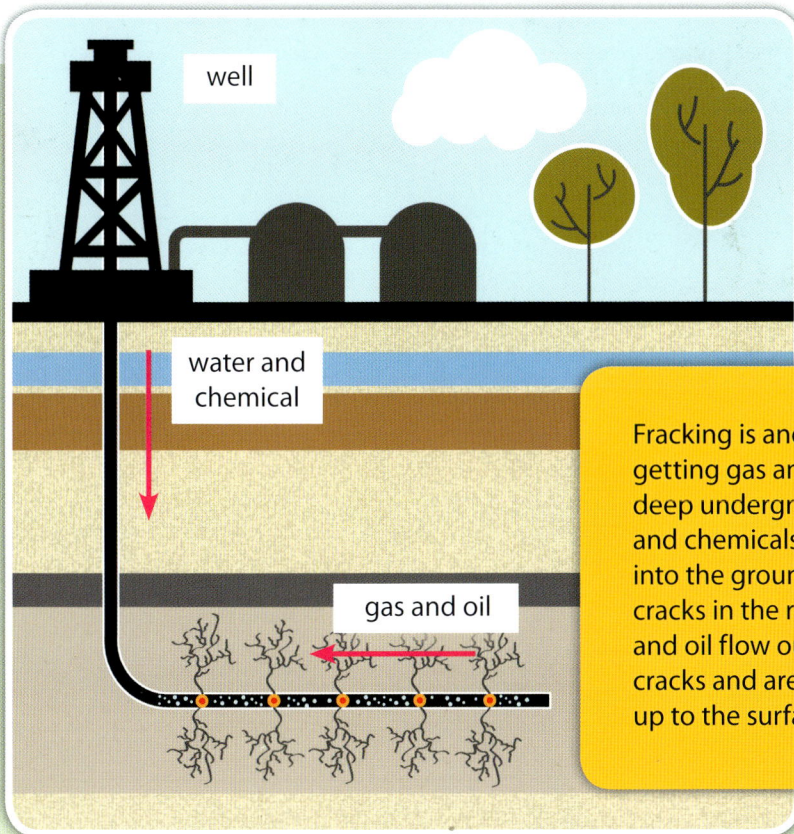

well

water and chemical

gas and oil

Fracking is another way of getting gas and oil from deep underground. Water and chemicals are put into the ground to make cracks in the rock. Gas and oil flow out of the cracks and are pumped up to the surface.

On the other side of the debate about fossil fuel and its future is the effect that burning fossil fuel has on the environment. When fossil fuels are burned, they release large amounts of a gas called carbon dioxide into Earth's atmosphere.

Carbon dioxide stops heat escaping out into space, and traps it close to Earth's surface. This trapped heat then causes Earth's climate to change. Most scientists believe that humans are causing this *climate change* by burning fossil fuel. There may be some major effects such as ice caps melting and sea levels rising.

Global temperature index

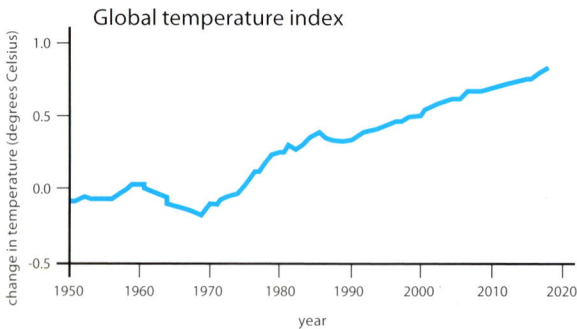

Source: NASA/GISS

Carbon dioxide index

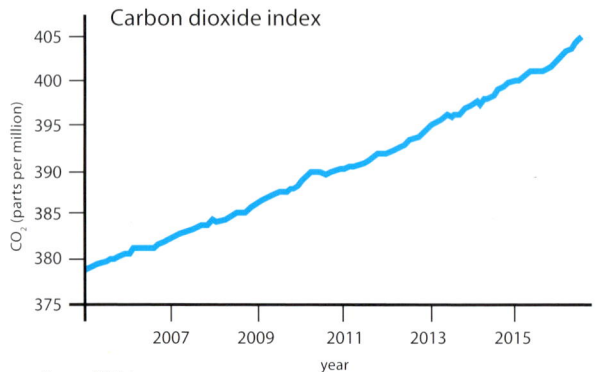

Source: NOAA

These graphs show that the average temperature of the world has risen by almost one degree Celsius since 1950, and that carbon dioxide levels are rising. Earth is heating up steadily.

Yet some people do not agree that humans are causing climate change by burning fossil fuel. They say that Earth naturally warms and cools at times. They say the carbon dioxide made by burning fossil fuel is absorbed, or taken in, by the sea and by large forests.

Fossil fuel contains a lot of carbon. When it is burned, it combines with oxygen to become carbon dioxide gas.

POWER FACT

Trees use and store carbon dioxide gas as they grow. Cutting down large forests can increase the amount of carbon dioxide in the air.

New power stations can use fossil fuel in a way that reduces the amount of carbon dioxide and other pollution it causes.

So, we can see that there is a big debate about fossil fuels and the future of energy. We know that we will need a lot of energy in the future. Earth's population is getting bigger. Many poorer countries are changing quickly and need increasing amounts of energy to do this.

The benefits of using fossil fuel for our energy needs are clear. Fossil fuel is quite easy to extract from Earth and to transport around the world. It burns well and releases lots of energy. Many people and businesses are looking to the future by developing new methods of extracting fossil fuel and by developing new ways of using it.

But there is a down side. More and more fossil fuel fields will run out, and new areas of land containing fossil fuel deposits may be more difficult and costly to use. New methods, such as tar sand mining, may cause a lot of environmental damage. The issue of climate change will also remain in the debate.

Therefore, scientists have been looking for other sources of energy. But what is there other than fossil fuel?

Is solar power the future of energy?

Solar power could play a large part in the future of energy. Solar power involves using the sun's energy to provide energy for many things. The most common ways of using the sun's energy are to heat things with it and to create electricity from it.

There are two ways of using the sun to make electricity. Solar thermal power stations have huge mirrors that focus the sun's energy onto *boilers* holding water. The water boils to produce steam, and the steam drives the machines that make electricity.

The ISEGS is one of the largest solar thermal power stations in the world. It lies in the Mojave Desert in California, USA.

We can also turn the sun's energy into electrical energy by building *solar cells* (PV cells). When sunlight hits these cells, it causes tiny particles called *electrons* to flow between thin layers. This flow creates electricity, which is then passed along wires to where it is needed.

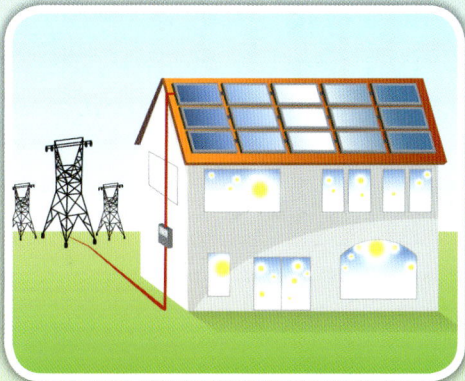

Solar PV cells can be put onto the roof of a house to provide electricity.

POWER FACT

Earth receives more solar energy in one hour than all energy people use in an entire year.

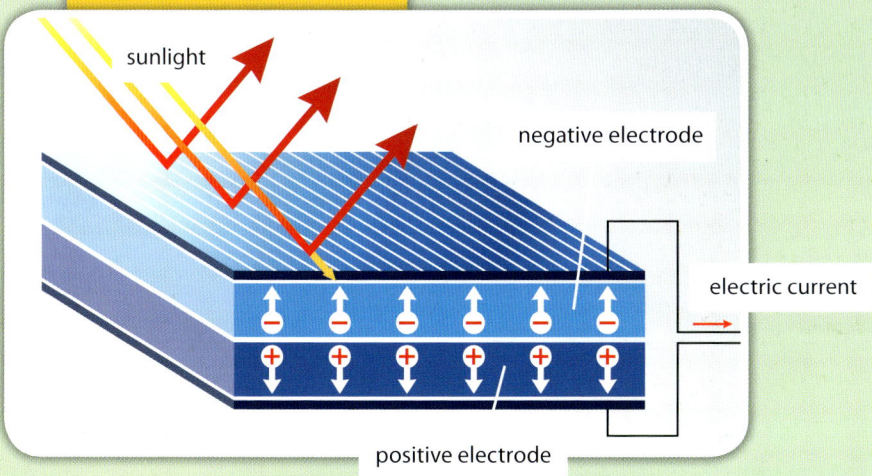

sunlight

negative electrode

electric current

positive electrode

We can already use the sun's energy to heat water for our homes by piping cold water through solar thermal panels that are attached to the roof. The panels capture the sun's heat and transfer it to the cold water, warming it up.

We can also design buildings that make as much use of receiving the sun's light and heat as possible. These passive solar buildings have large windows that face the sun. They are made from materials that absorb heat, and they have thick walls that stop heat escaping.

This passive solar building has been built to capture the sun's light and heat.

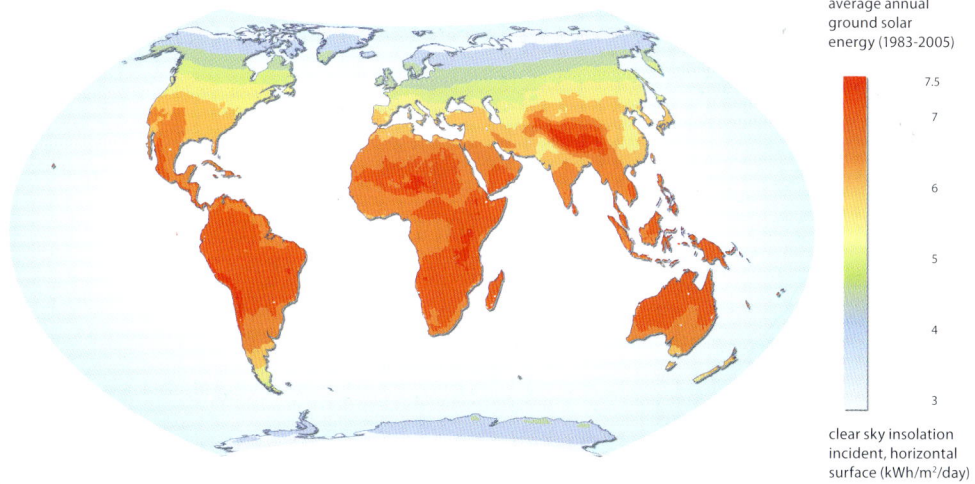

average annual ground solar energy (1983-2005)

7.5
7
6
5
4
3

clear sky insolation incident, horizontal surface (kWh/m²/day)

The red and orange places on this map show the parts of the world that get the most solar energy from the sun.

Of course, to get enough energy from solar power, we need enough sunlight. Solar power is not available during the night, when there is no sunlight. Solar thermal power stations and panels work best in parts of the world that get a lot of hot sunshine. Solar PV cells, however, can work even on cloudy days.

POWER FACT

Roughly one in seven homes in Australia have solar panels on their roofs to provide electricity.

There are many benefits of solar power. Because it can be used wherever there is sunlight, it can provide energy to remote places. These places do not need to be linked up to an *electricity grid*. Solar power also causes almost no pollution, and it is silent.

Solar power is a *renewable* source of energy. This means that we will never run out of it. And although solar thermal power stations, PV cells and thermal panels can be costly to make, sunlight is free.

Some people argue that solar panels are unattractive and ruin the landscape.

However, solar power is not as reliable as other sources of energy. There is no sunlight at night. And in many places, it is hard to predict when there will be thick cloud cover and less solar energy hitting Earth.

Some people are also concerned about the effects of large solar power farms on the environment. They take up a lot of ground and can change how the scenery looks.

POWER FACT

Almost 520,000 square kilometres of solar PV cells would be needed to create enough electricity to power the world. That area is roughly the size of Spain!

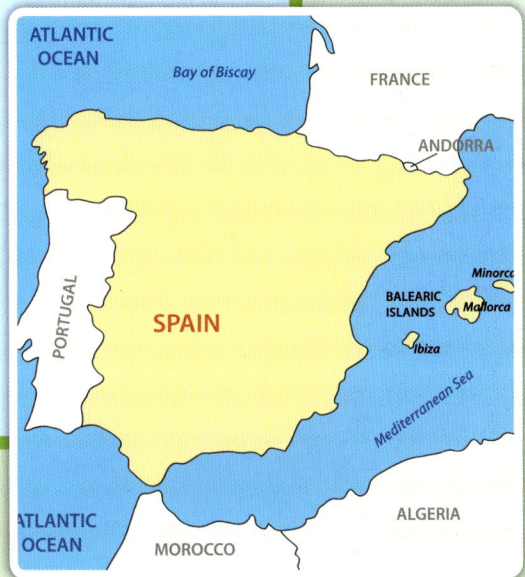

ATLANTIC OCEAN

Bay of Biscay

FRANCE

ANDORRA

PORTUGAL

SPAIN

BALEARIC ISLANDS

Minorca

Mallorca

Ibiza

Mediterranean Sea

ATLANTIC OCEAN

MOROCCO

ALGERIA

WHAT DO YOU THINK?

Is solar power a good option for the future of energy? Is it reliable enough? Could solar panels be used in snowy places?

Can the wind power our future?

The wind that blows through Earth's atmosphere is a type of *kinetic*, or movement, energy. Humans have used wind energy for thousands of years, to sail ships and to grind grain in windmills.

Today we can use the wind to create electricity in structures called wind *turbines*. Turbines are machines that spin when moving air, water or steam push against their blades. They are linked to machines called *generators*, which turn the spinning motion into electricity.

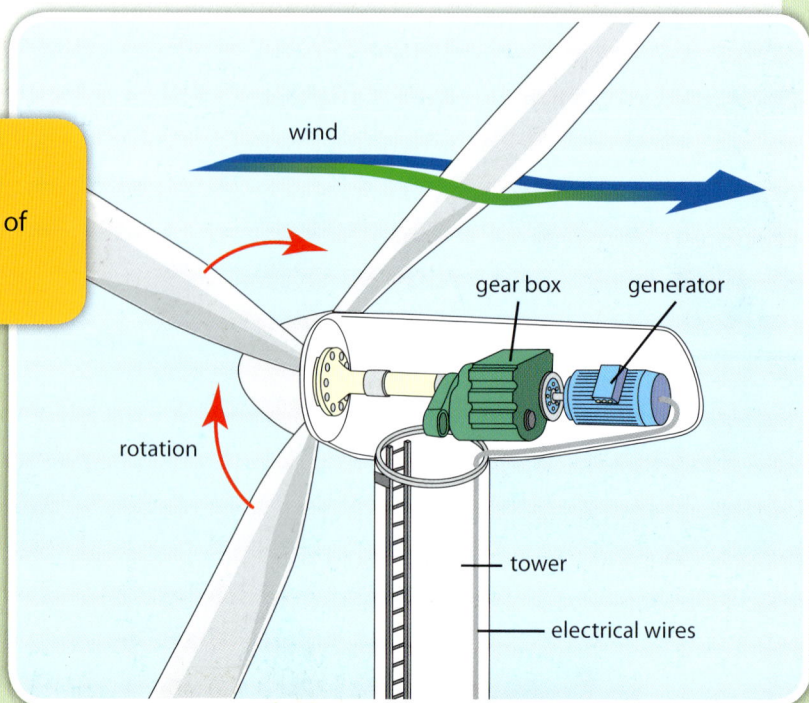

This diagram shows the parts of a wind turbine.

wind

gear box

generator

rotation

tower

electrical wires

Because the wind usually blows stronger high above the ground, large wind turbines are built on tall towers. One of the tallest in the world is in Germany. It stands at just over 230 metres tall!

Large groups of wind turbines are called wind farms. More wind farms are being built around the world, on land or out at sea.

The largest wind farm in the world is in the North Sea. When it is complete, it will have 300 huge wind turbines.

POWER FACT

Over one-third of the renewable energy in Australia is produced by wind farms.

Good sites for wind farms include places where wind can blow the strongest, such as out at sea, along the coast or on top of hills.

high land

coastal

sea

Many people believe that wind power is a good alternative to using fossil fuel. Like solar power, wind power is renewable. We won't run out of wind! And almost everywhere on Earth receives wind.

Yet some places are better for wind farms than others. Highland areas, coastal regions and sites out at sea are the best places. In these places, the wind blows at high speed and blows on most days. Even so, there are some times when the wind is not strong enough to turn the turbine blades and make electricity.

Although it is costly to build large wind farms, once they are built they provide very cheap electricity that does not create any air pollution. Small-scale wind farms, and even single wind turbines, can provide power to people in remote places.

The cost of making large wind turbines has fallen in recent years, making wind power more affordable than it used to be.

Although there are many good reasons to support wind power in the debate about energy, there are some other factors to think about. Wind power is clean and renewable, but large wind farms can create noise pollution as the giant blades turn through the air.

Many people also say that wind turbines destroy the beauty of natural places and that birds are in danger of being struck by the blades. Some people are even concerned that aircraft may fly into tall wind turbines.

POWER FACT

The largest wind turbines can each make about 8 *megawatts* of electricity. This is enough to provide power to around 10,000 homes. The smallest are light enough to be packed away and carried around and can make enough power to charge a phone.

WHAT DO YOU THINK?

Is wind power a better option than solar power? How does their reliability compare? Do the risks of fire or noise pollution outweigh the benefits of wind power?

Wind speed and direction can be unreliable, so wind turbines can't produce electricity all of the time. Also, some wind turbines have caught fire when the spinning blades caused the machines to overheat.

Wind turbine towers do not take up much space on the ground. Do you think wind turbines are ugly or elegant?

Can we create enough energy from water?

Water power plays a part in the debate about energy. We can take the kinetic energy of water and turn it into electrical energy.

On land, water flows because Earth's gravity is pulling it downhill. We can use this flowing movement to turn the blades on *hydroelectric*, water-powered, turbines. The turbines then turn generators, making electricity.

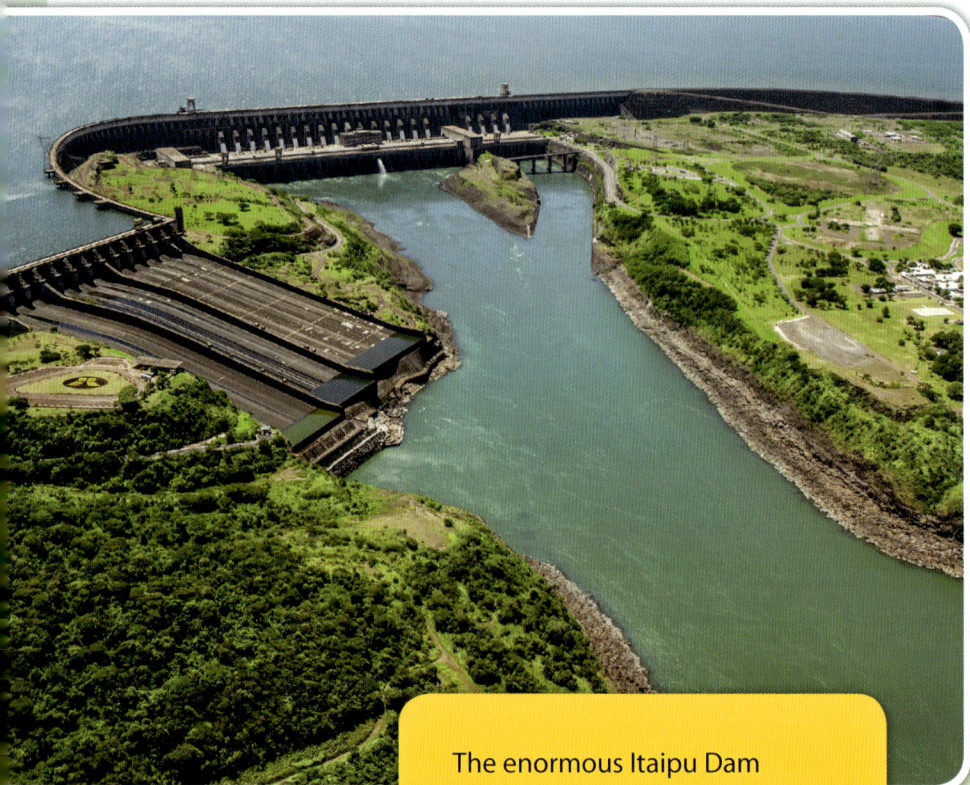

The enormous Itaipu Dam provides about 15 per cent of Brazil's electricity and about 75 per cent of Paraguay's electricity.

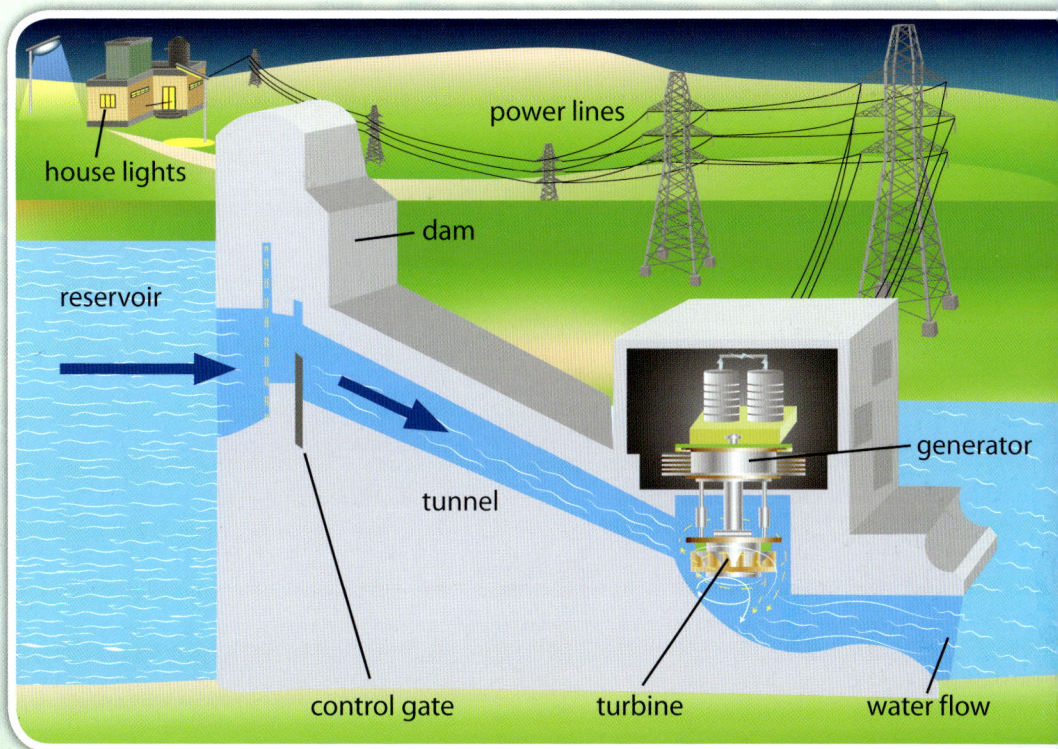

house lights

power lines

dam

reservoir

tunnel

generator

control gate

turbine

water flow

A cross-section diagram of an HEP dam shows how electricity travels to homes.

Around the world, people have built huge *dams* across rivers. These dams have hydroelectric power stations (HEPs) built inside them. When the tunnels in the dams are opened up, huge volumes of fast-flowing water drop through them. The water passes through turbines and makes large amounts of electricity. The electricity flows out along cables to where it is needed.

The water in the seas and oceans can also make electricity. Rising and falling *tides*, and the effect of waves, can turn turbines to make electricity.

The case for hydroelectricity is strong. It is a renewable form of energy, it causes very little pollution and the fuel it needs is free. About 71 per cent of Earth's surface is covered in water, so there are many places to make hydroelectricity.

Most rivers can be used to make electricity. Small rivers can be routed to flow through a turbine, and don't need to have dams. This means that water can supply local people with power in remote places.

Unlike solar and wind power, water power is very reliable. This is because rivers always flow (unless there is a drought and no rain falls). Tides rise and fall usually twice a day, and there are always some waves on the ocean surface.

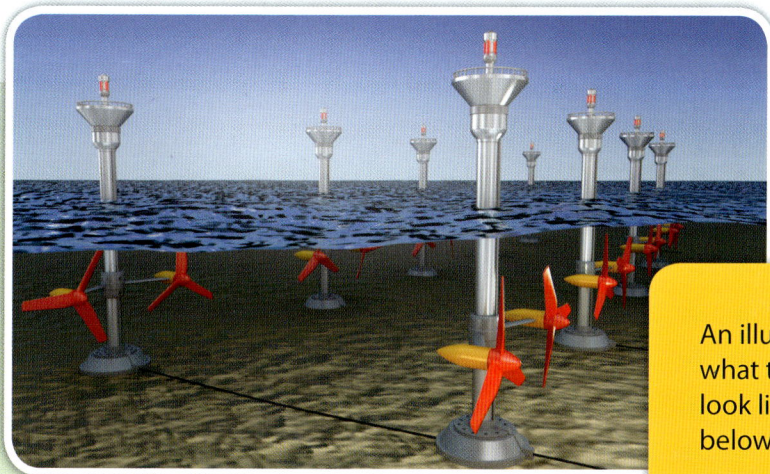

An illustration shows what turbines might look like above and below the water.

POWER FACT

The water held back behind a dam creates a large lake called a *reservoir*. The lake can be used to provide drinking water and can also be used for sports and hobbies.

But there are some issues to add to the debate about hydroelectricity. Most of these are about the huge dams that need to be built to provide enough electricity. The cost of building these dams is huge, and there are other negative factors.

The environmental effect of building a dam can be large. Huge pieces of land are lost as the land behind the dam floods. People have to leave their homes, and wildlife habitats are lost. The plant and animal life in the water is upset, as it can no longer move freely up or down the river. The dam can reduce or even stop the flow of the water down the river.

Some people are worried that tidal and wave power systems in the ocean might be a danger to ships. They may affect the sea life and may destroy the beauty of some coastlines.

WHAT DO YOU THINK?

Which type of water power do you think is best? Which type has the fewest drawbacks?

The site of the Old Petrolandia Church in Brazil was flooded for the construction of an HEP dam. It is all that remains of the city that used to stand here.

Is nuclear power the answer?

The place of *nuclear power* in the future of energy has been debated for many years. Nuclear power is the heat that is given out when a tiny particle called an *atom* is split apart. Everything is made of atoms, but some things are made of atoms that are very easy to split. So they are used as fuel in nuclear power stations to make electricity.

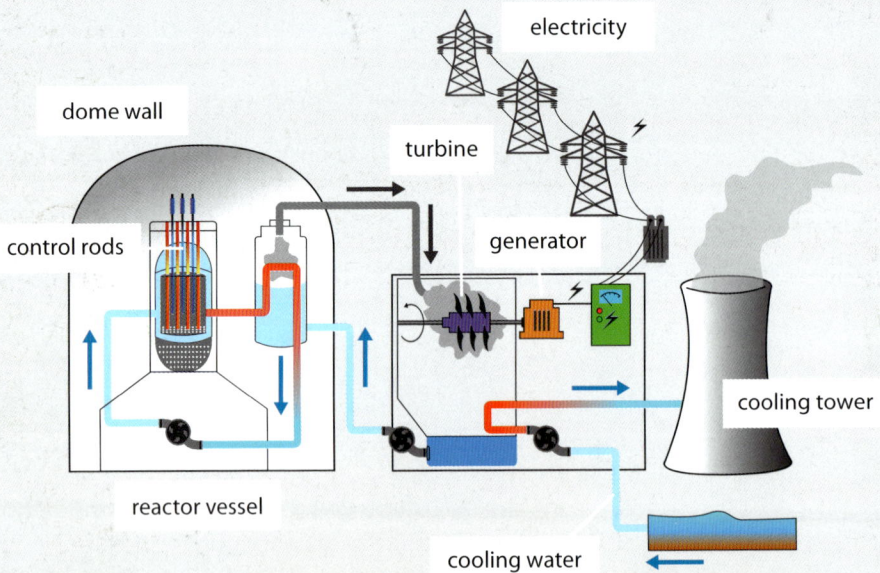

electricity

dome wall

turbine

control rods

generator

reactor vessel

cooling tower

cooling water

This diagram shows how a nuclear power station works. The water piped through the cooling towers helps to turn the steam back to water.

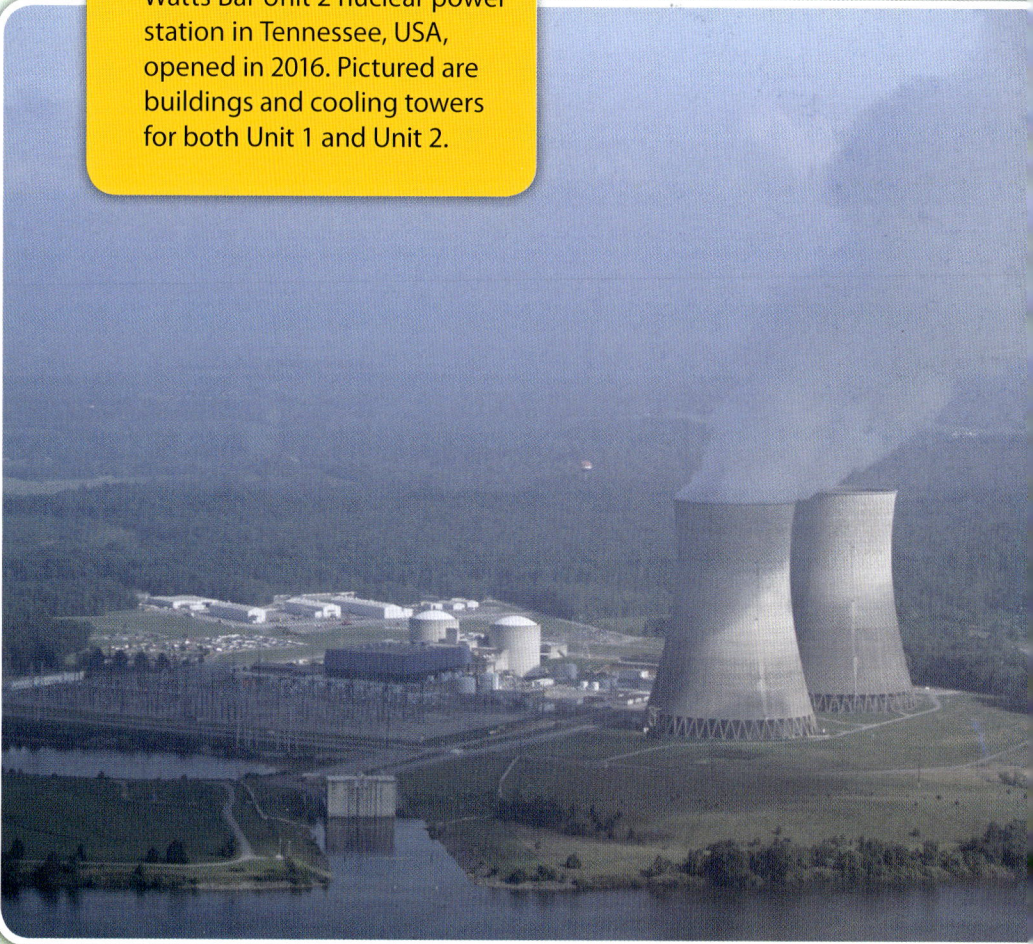

Watts Bar Unit 2 nuclear power station in Tennessee, USA, opened in 2016. Pictured are buildings and cooling towers for both Unit 1 and Unit 2.

In a nuclear power station, the fuel is placed into a *reactor* where the splitting of the atoms is controlled. This process is used to heat water. The water boils and makes steam. The steam turns a turbine connected to a generator, and electricity is made.

One of the main benefits of nuclear power is that it can supply electricity almost all of the time. This is unlike wind and solar power, which depend on the weather. Nuclear power does not create carbon dioxide, so it does not cause climate change.

Another good side of nuclear power is that the fuel it uses is very rich in energy. So only tiny amounts are needed to make lots of electricity. But the fuel is not renewable, and it will run out one day.

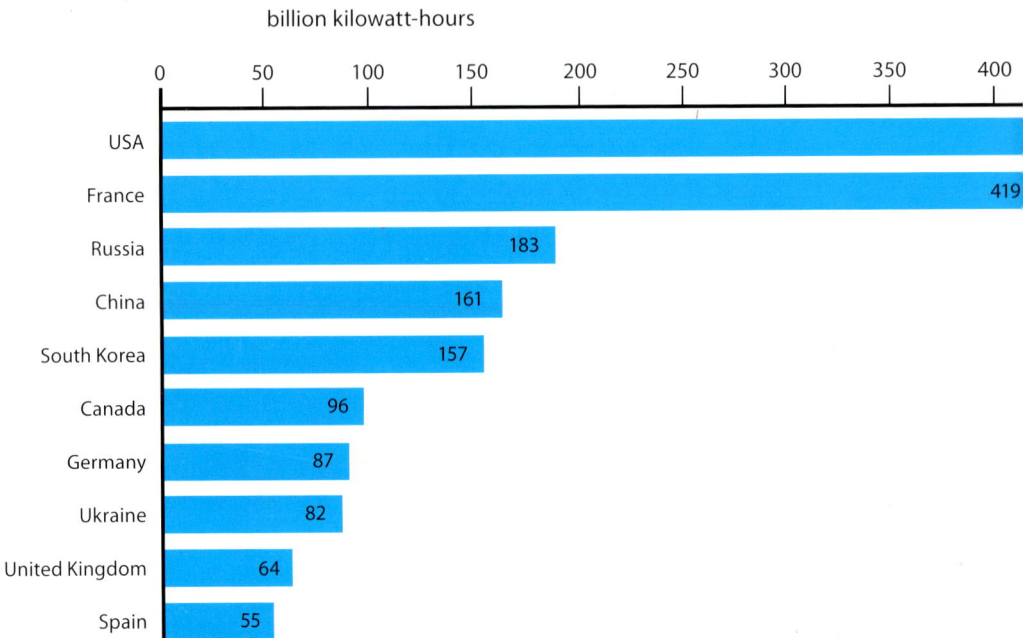

billion kilowatt-hours

Country	billion kilowatt-hours
USA	
France	419
Russia	183
China	161
South Korea	157
Canada	96
Germany	87
Ukraine	82
United Kingdom	64
Spain	55

Source: U.S. Energy Information Administration

The main factor in the debate about nuclear power is safety. When uranium atoms split, they give off *radiation*, or energy, as well as heat. Radiation can harm living things, causing diseases and death.

An explosion in 2011 at a Fukushima nuclear power plant in Japan released radiation into the water and air, which can cause cancer.

Nuclear electricity net generation 2015

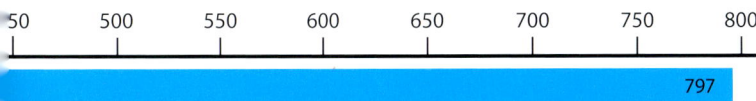

| 50 | 500 | 550 | 600 | 650 | 700 | 750 | 800 |

797

This graph shows the amount of nuclear energy that the countries generate. The amount is measured in billion kilowatt-hours. A kilowatt is a unit of power equal to 1,000 watts.

Building nuclear power stations is costly. This is because they must be very safe for the people who work there and live nearby. However, new technology means that they are now very safe, and they can also be built underground. Once built, they are cheap to run. So, although it seems that nuclear power is just too dangerous, it could be that it does have a future.

POWER FACT

Nuclear power provides about 11 per cent of the world's electricity today. There are 440 nuclear power stations in the world, spread across 31 countries.

WHAT DO YOU THINK?

Do you think the dangers of radiation mean that we should stop using nuclear energy? How else do you think we can make enough energy for a growing population?

A warning sign marks a closed uranium mine in Australia. Australia has 31 per cent of the world's uranium. But uranium will not last forever, and mining it can be harmful to the land.

Can Earth provide our energy?

Perhaps the answer to our future energy needs is just below our feet. Deep below Earth's surface is a layer of very hot, liquid rock called magma. This heats up the bottom layers of rock that form a hard crust around Earth. Where the crust is thin, water that seeps down can be heated by this hot rock. This is known as *geothermal energy*.

We can see geothermal energy in action where there are hot springs of water or geysers that shoot steam up out of the surface. We can also use this energy to heat buildings and make electricity.

In certain places, there is enough hot water to pipe it around buildings and heat them up. In other places, cold water is sent down pipes drilled down into Earth's crust, where it heats into steam. The steam is used to turn turbines and make electricity.

For geothermal power stations, most pipes are drilled down 600 to 3,000 metres into Earth's surface.

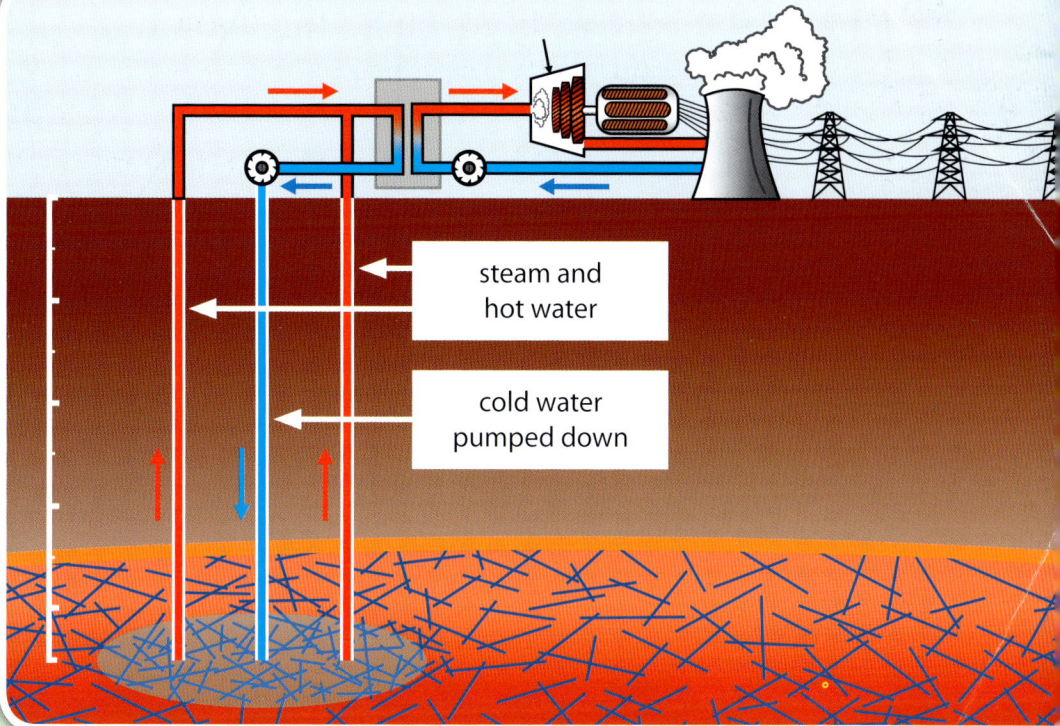

steam and hot water

cold water pumped down

POWER FACT

Over 50,000 times more energy exists in Earth's upper crust than the total energy from all the fossil fuels found on Earth.

Geothermal energy is renewable. There is so much heat in the earth that it will always manage to provide enough for our needs. Like nuclear power, it is possible to use geothermal energy almost all of the time, night and day. And once geothermal power stations and heating systems have been built, their running costs are very low.

The Krafla geothermal power plant is one of Iceland's largest power stations.

Older power stations had to be built only in places where the hot layers of rock were close to the surface. Now we can drill deeper. One day, geothermal energy may be possible to get from almost anywhere.

Even single buildings can use geothermal energy. Cold liquid sent down pipes drilled into the ground comes back up warmer. This warmth is used to heat water for the building.

Geothermal energy is a mainly safe and clean technology. Tourists swim in the hot springs right next to the power plant.

Geothermal power may sound like it might be the best option for our future energy needs. But there are some downsides to it that need to be thought about in the debate.

Although geothermal power stations don't create much pollution, some of them do give off harmful gases. The water that is brought from deep in Earth's crust can contain gases like carbon dioxide and methane. Yet most power stations now return these gases back down into the ground.

The water brought up from the crust can also contain tiny pieces of rock. This can damage pipes and other power station parts, so it needs to be removed. This is costly and takes time. But because the fuel is free the cost of geothermal energy is still very low.

Top five geothermal countries

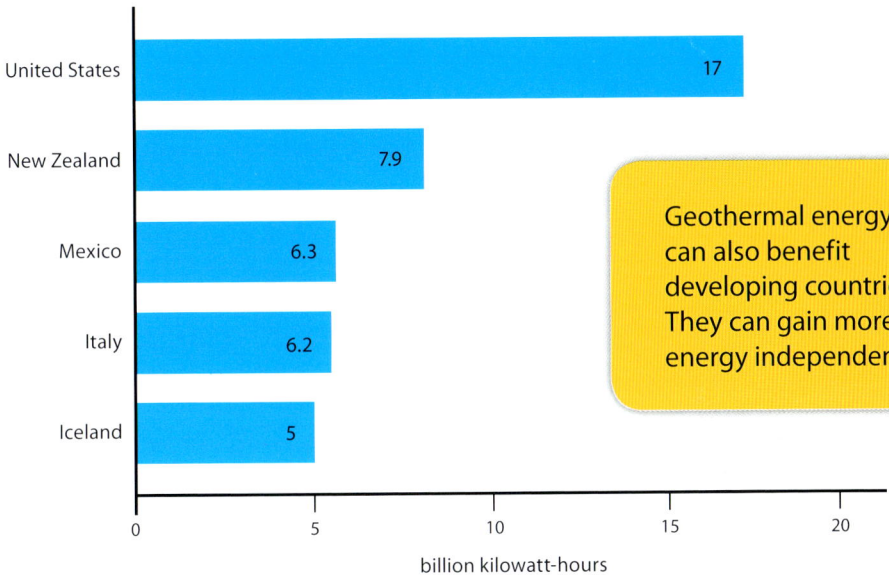

Country	billion kilowatt-hours
United States	17
New Zealand	7.9
Mexico	6.3
Italy	6.2
Iceland	5

billion kilowatt-hours

Source: U.S. Energy Information Administration

Geothermal energy can also benefit developing countries. They can gain more energy independence.

WHAT DO YOU THINK?

Drilling and building geothermal power stations are costly, but does the free fuel make geothermal energy a good option? Are there any places that can't use geothermal energy?

Are biomass and biogas the solution?

What if we could grow our own fuel? *Biomass* is the name given to fuel made from plants or waste products from plants and animals. Perhaps in the future we can grow enough biomass to provide our energy.

Around the world, many people use biomass every day to cook food and heat homes. The biomass fuel they use includes animal dung (droppings) and wood. But now there are crops only being grown to make biomass fuel for power stations. Some power stations also use waste products such as corn husks, sawdust, grass clippings, old tyres and even peanut shells! Many types of waste could one day be used as biomass fuel.

Power stations use the biomass to boil water to make steam. This turns turbines to make electricity.

Some biomass fuel is used in vehicle engines, instead of fossil fuels such as petrol or diesel. These biomass fuels are made from plants such as sugar cane, corn, wheat and soya beans.

Fast-growing switchgrass is a renewable resource that is used as a biomass fuel.

Biogas is a fuel made from rotting waste. When things rot, they give off a gas called methane. This gas can be captured and burned as biogas fuel. Waste food, animal dung and human sewage produce lots of methane. The waste is collected and left to rot in special tanks called *digesters*. Biogas can be burned in power stations to make electricity, or in homes for cooking and heating.

The large domes are the digesters at a biogas power station where waste is collected and processed for fuel.

Biomass and biogas will play a part in the future of energy. There are many things that could be used as biomass fuel, and making biogas is a great way to use waste. Biomass energy is renewable, because biomass crops can be replanted after they are picked. Biomass and biogas power stations can make electricity almost all the time, if they have enough fuel.

There are other benefits, too. Vehicles that use biofuels are better for the air than other vehicles. And many biomass crops provide good homes for wildlife and help to protect the soil.

POWER FACT

Energy from biomass and biogas makes up about 10 per cent of Earth's energy supply.

Like all the other energy sources for the future, there are some downsides to biomass and biogas energy. Many people are worried that growing biomass fuel will take up lots of land that should be used for growing food. This could make food more costly to buy and could cause people to go hungry in some countries. Growing large fields of biomass crops also uses a lot of water.

Like burning fossil fuels, burning biomass fuel gives off carbon dioxide. Although, if new crops are planted to make more biomass fuel, they will use up some of this carbon dioxide as they grow. This could mean that the carbon dioxide levels balance out.

This chart shows that generation of biomass energy is expected to continue to rise in the USA.

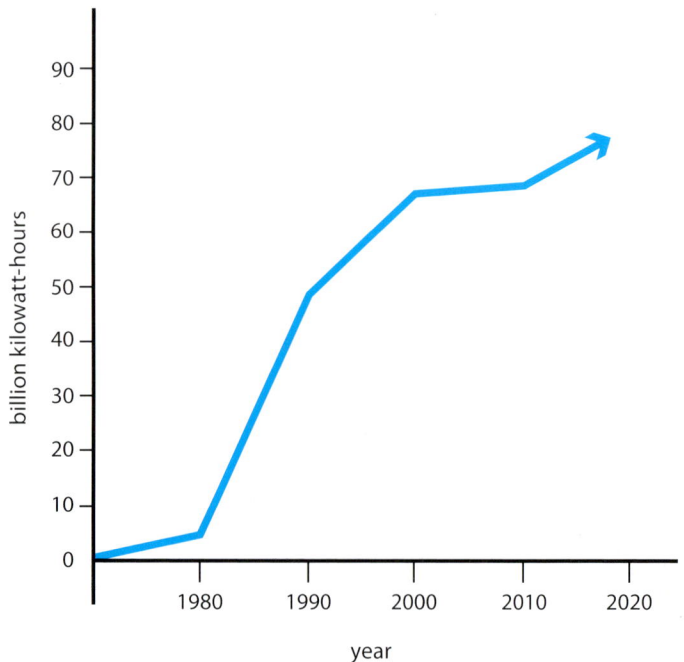

Source: U.S. Energy Information Administration

Land that is not good for growing food can be used to grow biofuel, such as an algae farm.

WHAT DO YOU THINK?

Why doesn't biomass fuel all vehicles? Do you think it should?

Should we change how we use energy?

The debate about the future of energy should not just be about how we get our energy. It should also be about how we use our energy. If we can use and waste less energy, we will be more *energy efficient*.

We can make buildings more energy efficient. We can do this by making small changes, for example by using energy-saving light bulbs. These use far less electricity than older kinds of light bulbs but give out the same amount of light. Larger changes could include using material called *insulation* in the roofs and walls of buildings to stop heat escaping.

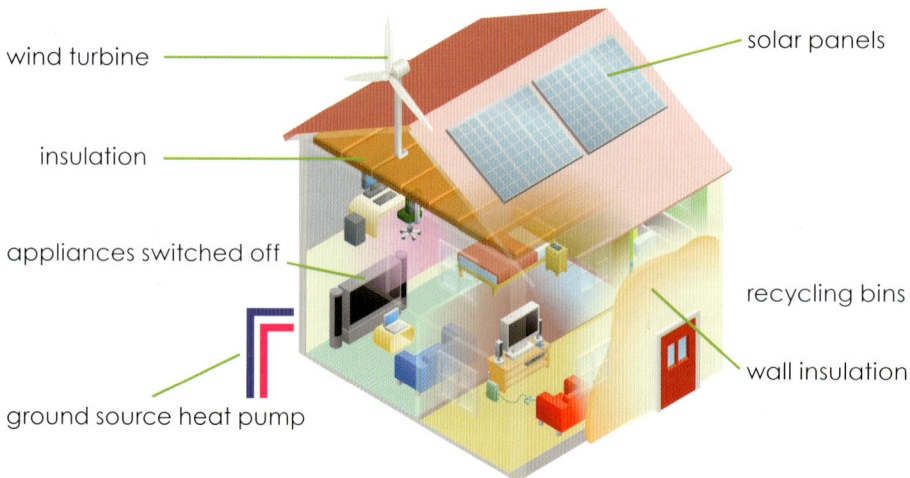

wind turbine

solar panels

insulation

appliances switched off

recycling bins

wall insulation

ground source heat pump

This diagram shows many ways of making a house more energy efficient.

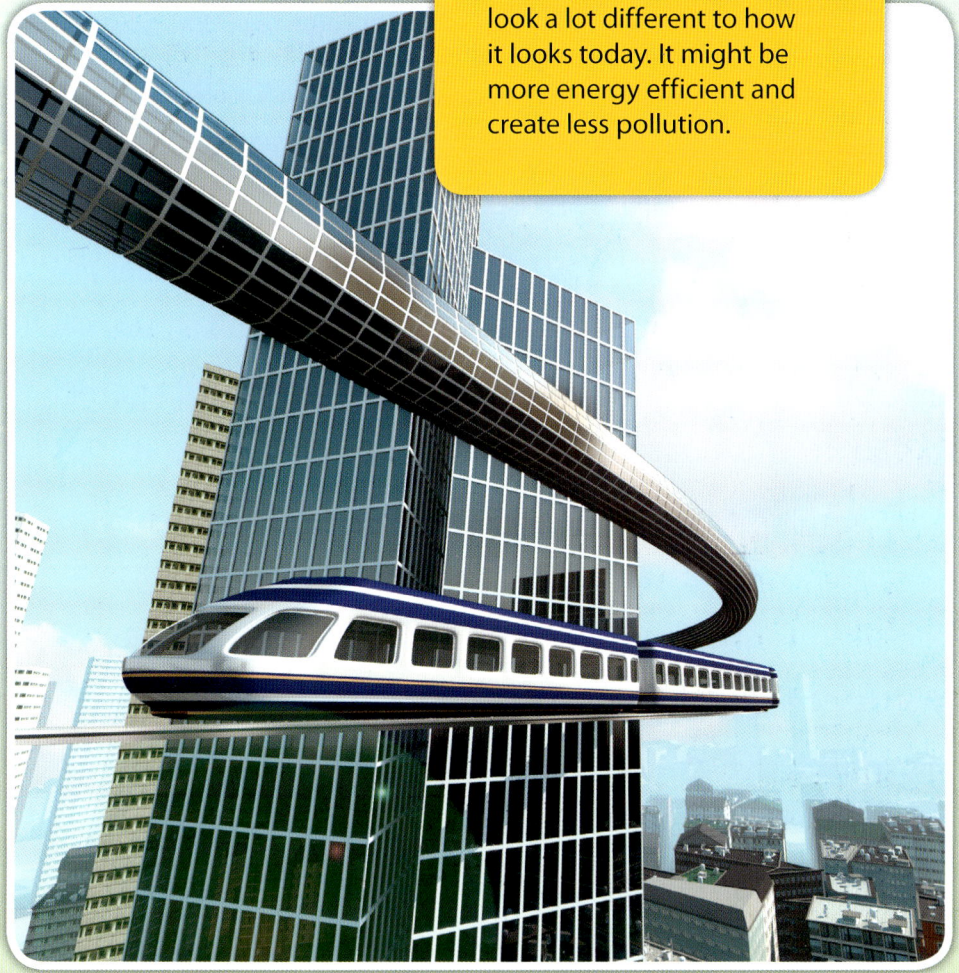

Future public transport may look a lot different to how it looks today. It might be more energy efficient and create less pollution.

Most modern vehicles now have engines that are very efficient and can travel further on one tank of fuel. Countries can spend money on improving their public transport systems, such as buses and trains. More people may use the improved systems, and there will be fewer cars on the roads.

The debate should also be about how we store energy. Lots of ways of making electricity in the future will rely on good ways of storing electricity.

For example, both solar power and wind power can only make electricity when there is enough sunlight or wind. When they do make electricity, sometimes not all of it is needed. So if the spare electricity can be stored, it can then be used when there is not enough sunlight or wind.

Another factor in the debate is the size of power stations. While we will always need large power stations, more and more small, local ways of making electricity will become important in the future. This will stop electricity being wasted as it travels in long power lines. If local areas make more than they need, they can connect to other electricity grids and send it there.

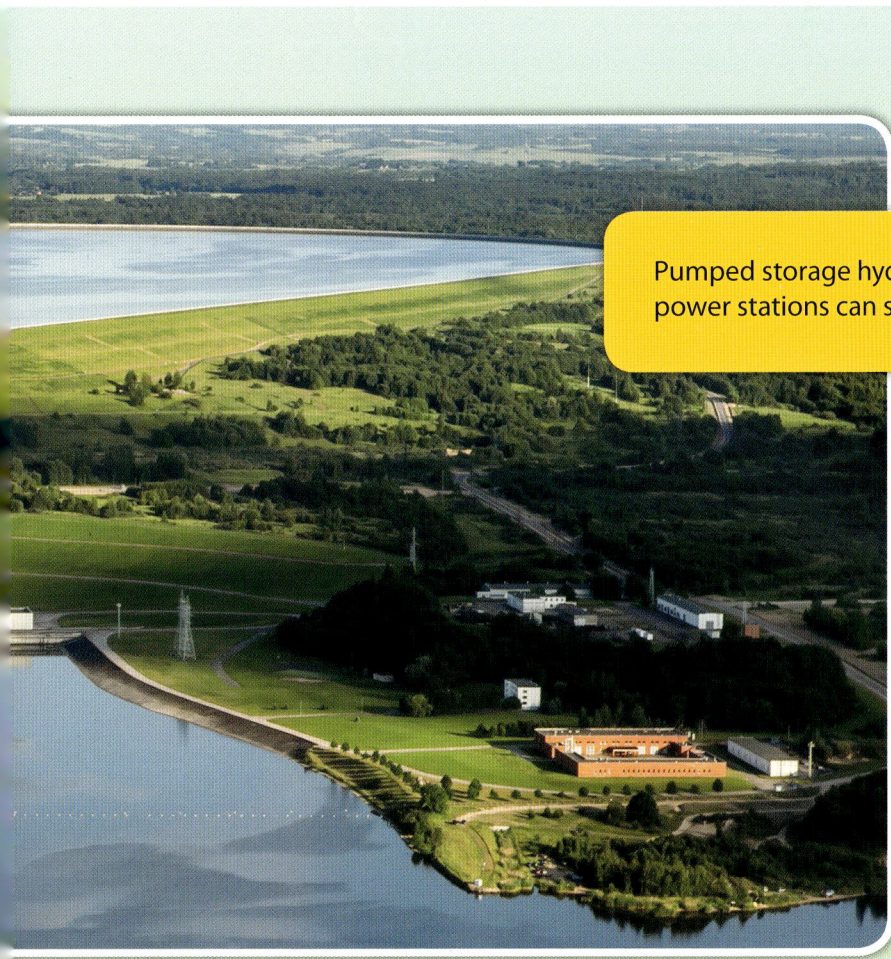

Pumped storage hydroelectric power stations can store energy.

Any debate about the future of energy should also include future knowledge. Many people today are working on new and better ways of capturing, storing and using energy.

Fuel cells can create electricity when two gases – hydrogen and oxygen – combine. They create no pollution, only water. There is a huge amount of hydrogen and oxygen in the world. So fuel cells are great inventions for the future.

New buildings can be made of materials that have solar PV cells built into them. And they can be painted with solar paint that captures the sun's energy. Solar clothing is also being made! This could use sunlight to power mobile phones. Smart clothing could also make electricity from the tiny movements made as you go about your daily life.

WHAT DO YOU THINK?

Do you think that electricity should be more costly for people in their homes and for businesses? Would this help people to use less electricity?

Fuel cell technology can be used in cars such as this one. People are working to make alternative energy better.

What is the future of energy?

The future of energy is a topic that people have been discussing for many years. The debate is sure to run for many more years!

The first part of the debate is about fossil fuels. How much is left? Can we find more? Even if we can, is it safe to keep burning fossil fuels? If we accept the link between burning fossil fuels and rising temperatures around the world, then we must accept that we have to find new sources of energy.

And what about these new sources of energy? What are their benefits? What are their downsides? It seems today that there isn't one simple solution that will provide enough power for all our needs. Perhaps in the future we will find new energy sources that will be the perfect solutions.

Rising temperatures around the world are causing problems for animals such as polar bears as polar ice melts.

The most likely outcome of the debate is that the future of energy will be a mixture of many solutions. We will keep using fossil fuel, and we will continue to look for new ways of extracting fossil fuel from Earth.

In the meantime, we will also keep using other energy sources – solar power, wind power, water power and nuclear power. We may also use geothermal power and biomass power. We will find better ways of using these energy sources and better ways of storing the electricity they can make.

Some energy options may be able to share the same space.

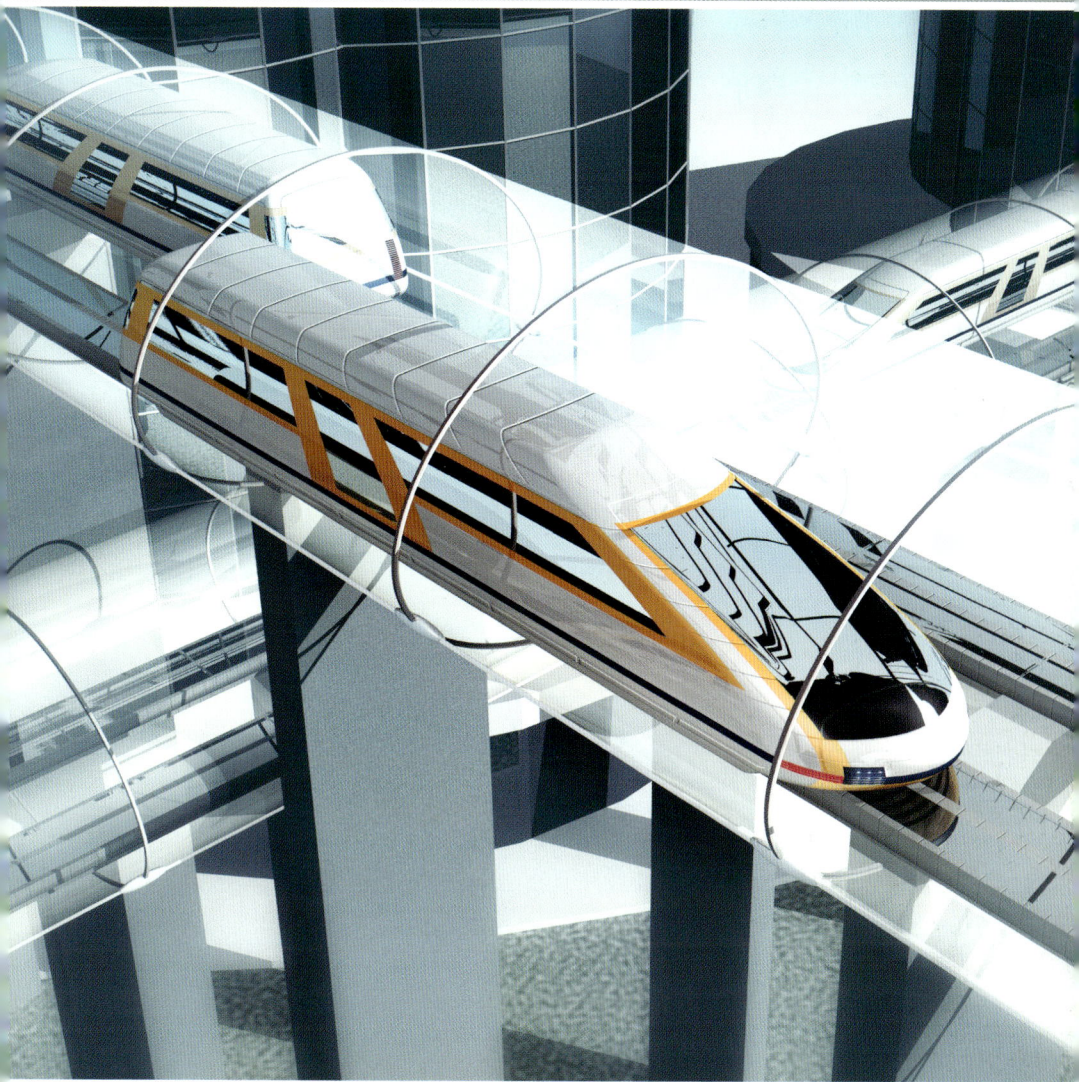

One day it might be possible to travel using new forms of energy.

The one thing we can do now is find ways of using energy better. We need to use less of it, and we need to use it more efficiently. We all need to think about small changes in our daily lives that will mean we use less energy. Added up, all these small changes will make a big difference.

Do you have any strong ideas about the future of energy? What do you think is the best type of energy to use?

Our future energy needs will be met by a mixture of different energy sources.

Glossary

atom tiny particle that is the building block for everything; each one is made up of protons, electrons and neutrons

biogas gas that is made when plant or animal wastes rot; it can be burned as fuel

biomass plants, waste products or animal wastes that are burned as fuel

boiler tank that boils water to make steam

climate change shift in Earth's weather patterns that affects the whole planet and happens slowly over time

dam wall built across a river that blocks the river's flow and causes water to flood behind it

digester tank for breaking down plant or animal materials

electricity grid network of paths for delivery of electric power

electron one of the tiny pieces of matter that make up all things; an electron travels around the nucleus of an atom.

energy efficient using less energy to do the same thing; not wasting energy

fossil fuel carbon-based fuel made from the remains of ancient plants and animals; it includes coal, oil and natural gas

fuel cell device that creates electricity through a chemical reaction between hydrogen and oxygen

generator machine that converts fuel or movement into electricity

geothermal energy heat energy from Earth, created below Earth's crust

hydroelectric having to do with electricity that is created by the movement of water

insulation material that stops heat, sound or cold from entering or getting out

kinetic having to do with movement or motion

megawatts unit for measuring electrical power; one megawatt is the rate at which about 1,000 homes use power

non-renewable not able to be made again in the time that it is needed; existing in a limited amount only

nuclear power power created by splitting atoms; atoms are the smallest part of a substance

power station building or place where electricity is made

radiation energy that is given out by certain materials, in the form of invisible electromagnetic waves

reactor large machine in which nuclear energy is produced by splitting atoms under controlled conditions

renewable able to be made again, or renewed; existing in unlimited amounts

reservoir large body of water, such as a lake, that collects behind a dam across a river

solar cell photovoltaic (PV) cell that converts sunlight into electrical energy and is used as a power source

solar power energy from the sun that can be used for heating and electricity

tide rising and falling of ocean water; tides move twice every day

turbine engine that has blades or paddles that spin when flowing air or liquid passes through it

Index